THE
BEST STANDARDS EVER

HAL LEONARD PUBLISHING CORPORATION

Home Office:
960 East Mark Street
Winona MN 55987

National Sales Office:
8112 West Bluemound Road
Milwaukee WI 53913

THE
BEST STANDARDS EVER

4

MAIRZY DOATS

By MILTON DRAKE, AL HOFFMAN,
and JERRY LIVINGSTON

Lightly

mf

F **C9** **F** **C9** **F** **C9** **F**

I know a dit-ty nut-ty as a fruit cake, goof-y as a goon and sil-ly as a loon.

Am **E9** **Am** **D7** **G7** **Edim** **G7** **C7** **Cdim** **C7**

Some call it pret-ty, oth-ers call it cra-zy, but they all sing this tune:

F **F#dim** **Gm7** **C7** **F** **C+**

mf

Mair-zy doats and do-zy doats and lid-dle lam-zy div-ey, a kid-dle-y div-ey too, would-n't you? Yes!

3

A MAN AND A WOMAN
(Un Homme Et Une Femme)

Original Words by PIERRE BAROUH
English Words by JERRY KELLER
Music By FRANCIS LAI

MANHATTAN
(From The Broadway Musical "GARRICK GAITIES")

Words by LORENZ HART
Music by RICHARD RODGERS

We'll have Man - hat - tan   The Bronx and Stat - en   Is - land too;_____ It's love - ly

We'll go to Green - wich   Where mod - ern men itch   to be free;_____ And Bowl - ing

We'll go to Yonk - ers   Where true love con - quers   in the wilds;_____ And starve to-

We'll have Man - hat - tan   The Bronx and Stat - en   Is - land too;_____ We'll try to

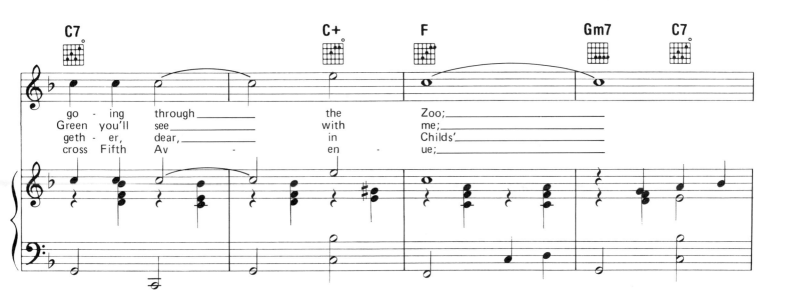

go - ing through _____ the   Zoo;_____

Green you'll see _____ with   me;_____

geth - er, dear, _____ in   Childs'

cross Fifth Av - _____ en - ue;_____

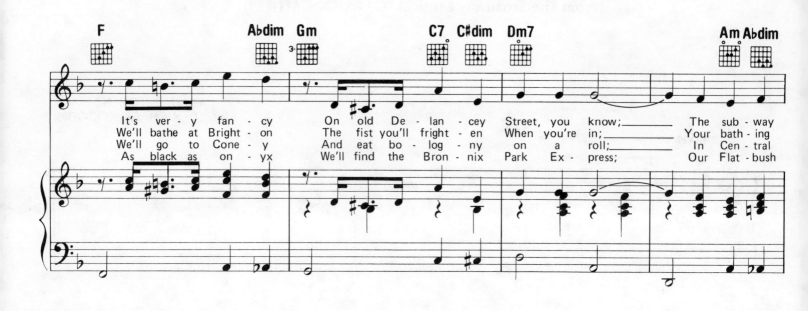

It's ver-y fan-cy On old De-lan-cey Street, you know;___ The sub-way
We'll bathe at Bright-on The fist you'll fright-en When you're in;___ Your bath-ing
We'll go to Cone-y And eat bo-log-ny on a roll;___ In Cen-tral
As black as on-yx We'll find the Bron-nix Park Ex - press; Our Flat-bush

charms us so,___ When balm-y breez-es blow to and fro; And tell me what street
suit so thin___ Will make the shell-fish grin Fin to fin; I'd like to take a
Park, we'll stroll___ Where our first kiss we stole, Soul to soul; And for some high fare
flat, I guess___ Will be a great suc-cess. More or less; A short va-ca-tion

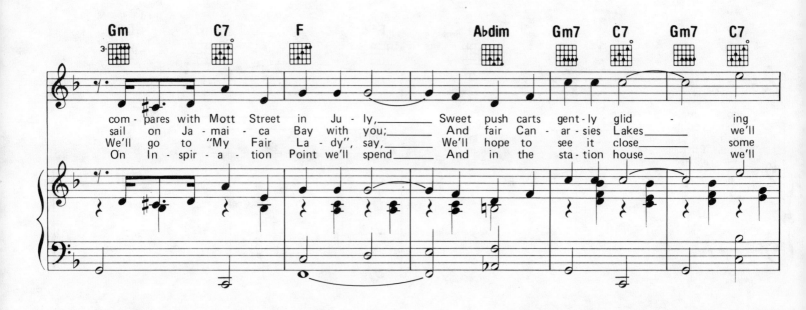

com-pares with Mott Street in Ju - ly,___ Sweet push carts gent-ly glid - ing
sail on Ja-mai - ca Bay with you;___ And fair Can - ar-sies Lakes___ we'll
We'll go to "My Fair La - dy", say,___ We'll hope to see it close___ some
On In - spir-a - tion Point we'll spend___ And in the sta-tion house___ we'll

MEDITATION

English Words by NORMAN GIMBEL
Original Words by NEWTON MENDONCA
Music by ANTONIO CARLOS JOBIM

MCA MUSIC

MISTY

Words by JOHNNY BURKE
Music by ERROLL GARNER

Slowly, with expression

Look at me, I'm as help-less as a kit-ten up a tree And I feel like I'm

cling-ing to a cloud, I can't __ un-der-stand, __ I get mist-y just hold-ing your

hand. __ Walk my way and a

Lyrics:

That's why I'm fol-low-ing you. On my own, would I wan-der through this won-der-land a - lone, Nev-er know-ing my right foot from my left, My hat from my glove, I'm too mist-y and too much in love.

Look at love.

MOONLIGHT AND ROSES
(Bring Mem'ries Of You)

Words and Music by
BEN BLACK & NEIL MORET

MOONLIGHT COCKTAIL

By LUCKY ROBERTS
and KIM GANNON

MORE
(Theme From MONDO CANE)

English Words by NORMAN NEWELL
Music by R. ORTOLANI and N. OLIVIERO

More than the great-est love the world has known;

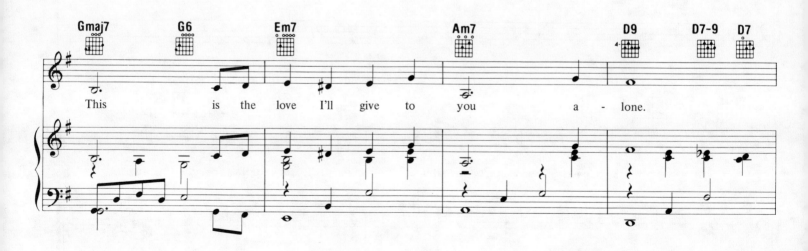

This is the love I'll give to you a - lone.

23

MR. WONDERFUL
(From the Musical "MR. WONDERFUL")

Words and Music by JERRY BOCK,
LARRY HOLOFCENER and GEORGE WEISS

Slowly and expressively

MY FUNNY VALENTINE
(From "BABES IN ARMS")

Words by LORENZ HART
Music by RICHARD RODGERS

MY WAY

Orignial French Lyric by GILLES THIBAULT
Music by CLAUDE FRANCOIS and JACQUES REVAUX
English Lyric by PAUL ANKA

MCA MUSIC

NEVERTHELESS
(I'm In Love With You)

Words and Music by
BERT KALMAR and HARRY RUBY

NICE WORK IF YOU CAN GET IT

(From "DAMSEL IN DISTRESS")

Words by IRA GERSHWIN
Music by GEORGE GERSHWIN

OL' MAN RIVER
(From "SHOW BOAT")

Words by OSCAR HAMMERSTEIN II
Music by JEROME KERN

OLD CAPE COD

Words and Music by CLAIRE ROTHROCK,
MILT YAKUS and ALLAN JEFFREY

Slowly, with expression

OLD DEVIL MOON

(From "FINIAN'S RAINBOW")

Words by E. Y. HARBURG
Music by BURTON LANE

ONE OF THOSE SONGS

Words by WILL HOLT
Music by GERALD CALVI

MCA MUSIC

OUR DAY WILL COME

Words by BOB HILLIARD
Music by MORT GARSON

Slowly, with expression

51

OUR LANGUAGE OF LOVE
(From "IRMA LA DOUCE")

Music by MARGUERITE MONNOT
Original French words by ALEXANDRE BREFFORT
English words by JULIAN MORE,
DAVID HENEKER and MONTY NORMAN

THE PARTY'S OVER

(From "BELLS ARE RINGING")

Words by Betty Comden
and Adolph Green
Music by Jule Styne

MCA MUSIC

PEOPLE

(From "FUNNY GIRL")

Words by BOB MERRILL
Music by JULE STYNE

PEOPLE WILL SAY WE'RE IN LOVE

(From "OKLAHOMA!")

Words by OSCAR HAMMERSTEIN II
Music by RICHARD RODGERS

RED ROSES FOR A BLUE LADY

By SID TEPPER
and ROY C. BENNETT

SATIN DOLL

By DUKE ELLINGTON,
JOHNNY MERCER and BILLY STRAYHORN

SOME ENCHANTED EVENING
(From "SOUTH PACIFIC")

Words by OSCAR HAMMERSTEIN II
Music by RICHARD RODGERS

SEEMS LIKE OLD TIMES

Words and Music by JOHN JACOB LOEB
and CARMEN LOMBARDO

SEPTEMBER SONG
(From the Musical Play "KNICKERBOCKER HOLIDAY")

Words by MAXWELL ANDERSON
Music by KURT WEILL

SHE LOVES ME
(From the Musical "SHE LOVES ME")

Words by SHELDON HARNICK
Music by JERRY BOCK

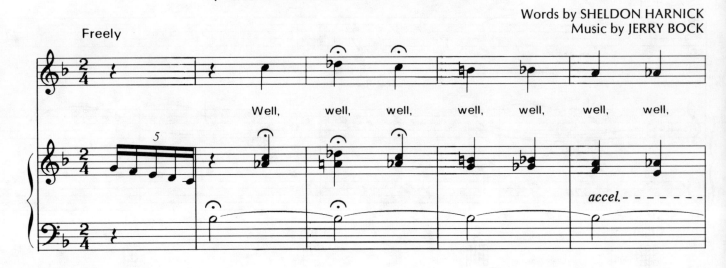

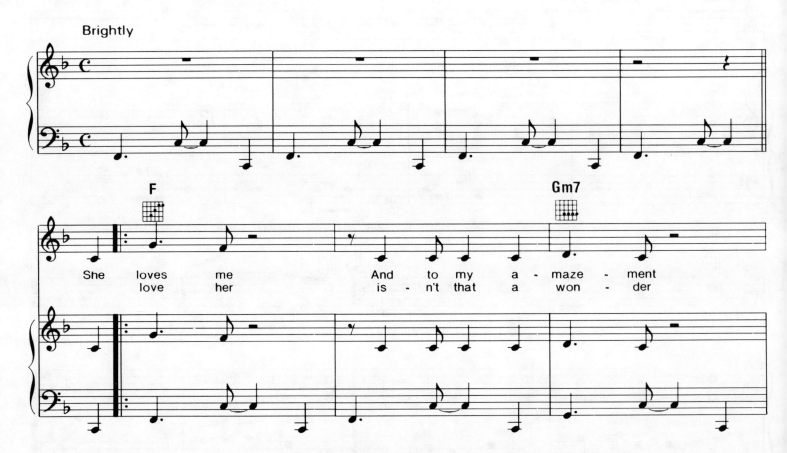

THE SHEIK OF ARABY

Words by HARRY B. SMITH
and FRANCIS WHEELER
Music by TED SNYDER

SMALL WORLD
(From "GYPSY")

Words by STEPHEN SONDHEIM
Music by JULE STYNE

SO IN LOVE
(From "KISS ME KATE")

Words and Music by COLE PORTER

Strange, dear, _____ but true, dear, _____ When

I'm close _____ to you, dear, _____ The

SOMETIMES I'M HAPPY

Words by CLIFFORD GREY and LEO ROBIN
Music by VINCENT YOUMANS

SPEAK LOW

(From "ONE TOUCH OF VENUS")

Words by OGDEN NASH
Music by KURT WEILL

STRANGERS IN THE NIGHT

Words by CHARLES SINGLETON
and EDDIE SNYDER
Music by BERT KAEMPFERT

MCA MUSIC

STAY AS SWEET AS YOU ARE

Words by MACK GORDON
Music by HARRY REVEL

A STRING OF PEARLS

Words by EDDIE DELANGE
Music by JERRY GRAY

SUGAR BLUES

Words by LUCY FLETCHER
Music by CLARENCE WILLIAMS

Moderate Blues tempo

Piano

Vamp

Verse

Have you   heard   these blues _____   that I'm going to sing to you? _____
I just   love   sweet food, _____   puts me in a nice sweet mood. _____

When you hear them,   they will thrill you thru and
When I'm like that,   you will nev-er find me

112

SUMMERTIME
(From "PORGY AND BESS")

Words by DuBOSE HEYWARD
Music by GEORGE GERSHWIN

A SUNDAY KIND OF LOVE

Words and Music by BARBARA BELLE,
LOUIS PRIMA, ANITA LEONARD and STAN RHODES

SUNRISE, SUNSET
(From the Musical "FIDDLER ON THE ROOF")

Words by SHELDON HARNICK
Music by JERRY BOCK

120

THE SWEETEST SOUNDS
(From "NO STRINGS")

Words and Music by
RICHARD RODGERS

THERE'S A SMALL HOTEL
(From "ON YOUR TOES")

Words by LORENZ HART
Music by RICHARD RODGERS

TAMMY

Words and Music by JAY LIVINGSTON
and RAY EVANS

Moderately

mp   *mp* rit.

Tenderly

Eb   Gm   Ab   Eb

I hear the cot - ton - woods whis - p'rin' a - bove:
Whip - poor - will, whip - poor - will, you and I know,

mp

Gm   Cm   Fm   Bb7   Eb

Tam - my! Tam - my! Tam - my's {my / in} love! The ole hoot - ie
Tam - my! Tam - my! Can't let him go! The breeze from the

Gm   Ab   Eb   Gm   Ab

owl hoot - ie - hoo's to the dove: Tam - my! Tam - my!
bay - ou keeps mur - mur - ing low: Tam - my! Tam - my!

129

THAT'S LIFE

Words and Music by DEAN KAY
and KELLY GORDON

THEY ALL LAUGHED

Words by IRA GERSHWIN
Music by GEORGE GERSHWIN

136

THEY CAN'T TAKE THAT AWAY FROM ME

Words by IRA GERSHWIN
Music by GEORGE GERSHWIN

With movement

THIS COULD BE
THE START OF SOMETHING

Words and Music by STEVE ALLEN

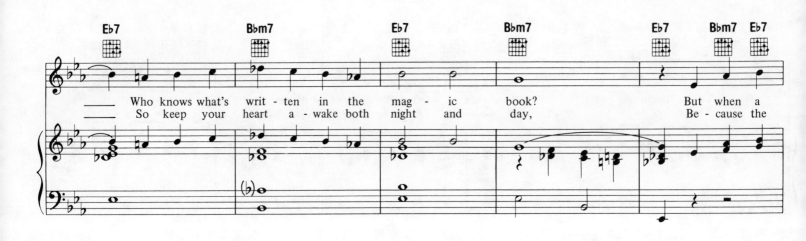

Who knows what's writ - ten in the mag - ic book? But when a
So keep your heart a - wake both night and day, Be - cause the

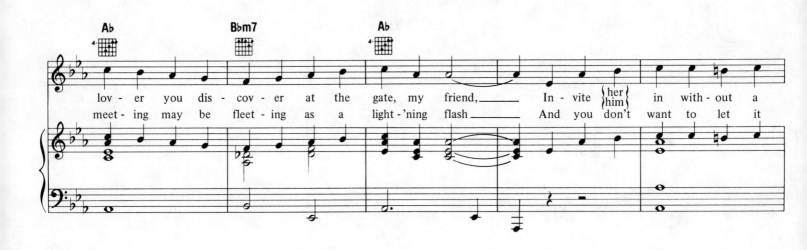

lov - er you dis - cov - er at the gate, my friend, In - vite {her}{him} in with - out a
meet - ing may be fleet - ing as a light - 'ning flash And you don't want to let it

sec - ond look! You're up in an aer - o - plane, or din - ing at
slip a way! You're watch - ing the sun come up, or count - ing your

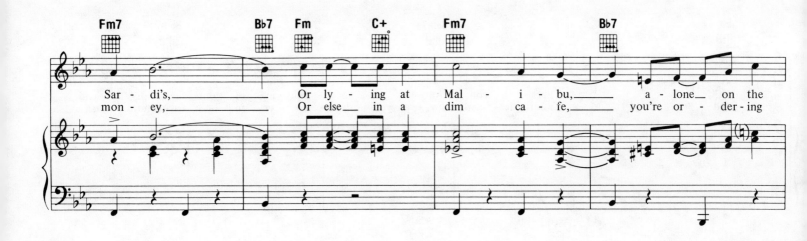

Sar - di's, Or ly - ing at Mal - i - bu, a - lone on the
mon - ey, Or else in a dim ca - fe, you're or - der - ing

THOROUGHLY MODERN MILLIE
(From Ross Hunter's "THOROUGHLY MODERN MILLIE" - A Universal Picture)

Words by SAMMY CAHN
Music by JAMES VAN HEUSEN

TILL

Words by CARL SIGMAN
Music by CHARLES DANVERS

'TIL TOMORROW
(From the Musical "FIORELLO!")

Words by SHELDON HARNICK
Music by JERRY BOCK

153

TOO CLOSE FOR COMFORT

(From the Musical "MR. WONDERFUL")

Words and Music by JERRY BOCK,
LARRY HOLOFCENER and GEORGE WEISS

UNDECIDED

Words by SID ROBIN
Music by CHARLES SHAVERS

MCA MUSIC

160

TRUE LOVE

Moderately Slow

Words and Music by
COLE PORTER

TRY TO REMEMBER
(From "THE FANTASTICKS")

Words by TOM JONES
Music by HARVEY SCHMIDT

Slowly, with tenderness

VAYA CON DIOS
(MAY GOD BE WITH YOU)

Words and Music by LARRY RUSSELL,
INEZ JAMES and BUDDY PEPPER

Moderate Waltz Tempo

THE WAY YOU LOOK TONIGHT

Words by DOROTHY FIELDS
Music by JEROME KERN

WHEN THE RED, RED ROBIN COMES BOB, BOB BOBBIN' ALONG

By HARRY WOODS

Moderately, with a bounce

When The

Red, Red Rob - in Comes Bob, Bob, Bob-bin' A - long, a -

long, There'll be no more sob - bin' when he starts throb-bin' his

old, sweet song. Wake up, wake

174

WHEN I FALL IN LOVE

Words by EDWARD HEYMAN
Music by VICTOR YOUNG

WHERE OR WHEN
(From "BABES IN ARMS")

Words by LORENZ HART
Music by RICHARD RODGERS

WHO'S SORRY NOW

Words by BERT KALMAR & HARRY RUBY
Music by TED SNYDER

WISH YOU WERE HERE
(From the musical "WISH YOU WERE HERE")

Words and Music by HAROLD ROME

THE WORLD IS WAITING FOR THE SUNRISE

Words by EUGENE LOCKHART
Music by ERNEST SEITZ

col 8va

YOU DON'T BRING ME FLOWERS

Words by NEIL DIAMOND, MARILYN BERGMAN
and ALAN BERGMAN
Music by NEIL DIAMOND

YESTERDAY'S SONGS

Words and Music by NEIL DIAMOND

(Say-in' I love you, now, ba-by, say-in' I love you, now, ba-by.)

Yes-ter-day's songs don't stay a-round long, not much an-y-more.
Yes-ter-day's songs don't seem to be-long. They're here, and they're gone.

Yes-ter-day's words don't make them-selves heard like they did be-fore.
Yes-ter-day's moves don't stay in the grooves. They keep mov-in' on.

YESTERDAYS

Words by OTTO HARBACH
Music by JEROME KERN

YOU NEEDED ME

Words and Music by RANDY GOODRUM

Moderately

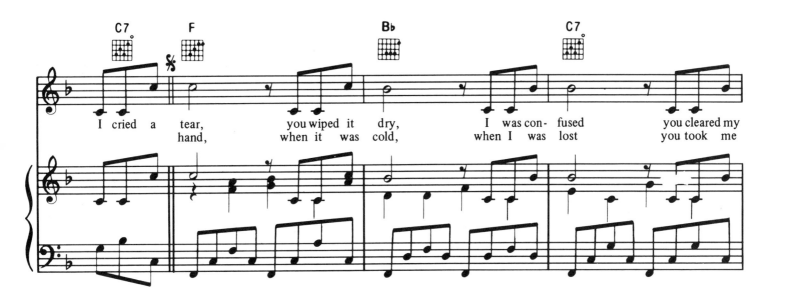

I cried a tear, you wiped it dry,
I was con-fused you cleared my
hand, when it was cold, when I was lost you took me

mind, I sold my soul, and held me
home You gave me hope, you bought it back for me and turned my
when I was at the end

YOU'D BE SO NICE TO COME HOME TO
(From "SOMETHING TO SHOUT ABOUT")

Words and Music by COLE PORTER

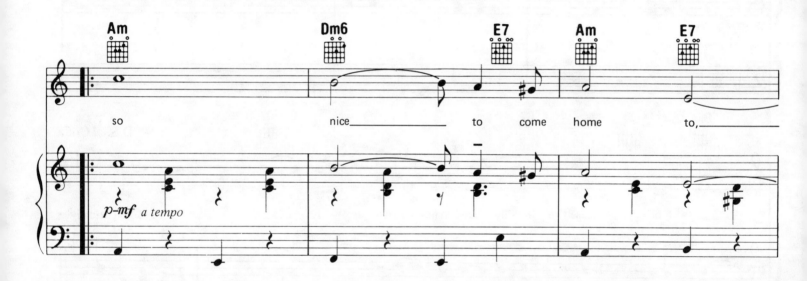

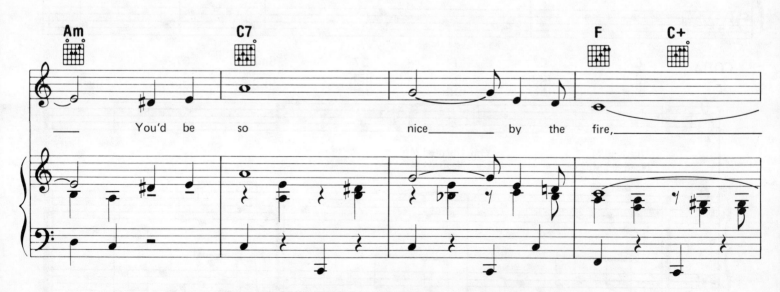

202

YOUNGER THAN SPRINGTIME
(From "SOUTH PACIFIC")

Words by OSCAR HAMMERSTEIN II
Music by RICHARD RODGERS

205

ZIP-A-DEE-DOO-DAH
(From Walt Disney's "SONG OF THE SOUTH")

Words by RAY GILBERT
Music by ALLIE WRUBEL

Piano/Vocal MIXED FOLIOS
Presenting the best variety of piano/vocal folios. Music includes guitar chord frames.

BEST BROADWAY SONGS EVER 00309155
Over 70 tunes featuring: All The Things You Are • Bewitched • Don't Cry For Me Argentina • I Could Have Danced All Night • If Ever I Would Leave You • Memory • Ol' Man River • You'll Never Walk Alone • and many more.

BEST CONTEMPORARY SONGS — 50 Top Hits 00359190
Some of the best, most recent hits, featuring: Any Day Now • Deja Vu • Endless Love • Flashdance. . . What A Feeling • I.O.U. • Islands In The Stream • September Morn • Through The Years • You Needed Me • and many more.

THE BEST COUNTRY SONGS EVER 00359498
79 all-time country hits including: Always On My Mind • Could I Have This Dance • God Bless The U.S.A. • Help Me Make It Through The Night • Islands In The Stream • and many more.

THE BEST EASY LISTENING SONGS EVER 00359193
Over 100 beautiful songs including: Around The World • Candle On The Water • Day By Day • A Foggy Day • I'll Never Smile Again • Just In Time • Manhattan • Strangers In The Night • and many more.

BEST KNOWN LATIN SONGS 00359194
A fabulous selection of over 50 favorite Latin songs including: Blame It On The Bossa Nova • A Day In The Life Of A Fool • The Girl From Ipanema • Poinciana • Quando, Quando, Quando • Spanish Eyes • Watch What Happens • Yellow Days • and many more!

THE BEST SONGS EVER 00359224
75 all-time hits including: Climb Ev'ry Mountain • Edelweiss • Feelings • Here's That Rainy Day • I Left My Heart In San Francisco • Love Is Blue • People • Stardust • Sunrise, Sunset • Woman In Love • many more.

THE BEST STANDARDS EVER Volume 1 00359231
and Volume 2 00359232
A two volume collection of 140 vintage and contemporary standards including: All The Things You Are • Endless Love • The Hawaiian Wedding Song • I Left My Heart In San Francisco • Misty • My Way • Old Cape Cod • People • Wish You Were Here • Yesterday's Songs • and many more.

THE BIG BAND ERA 00359260
Over 90 top songs from the time of the big bands including: Harbor Lights • I Can't Get Started • In The Mood • Juke Box Saturday Night • Moonglow • Paper Doll • String Of Pearls • Tuxedo Junction • Amapola • Jersey Bounce • and many more.

THE BIG 80 SONGBOOK 00359265
80 Recent hits and favorite standards including: Autumn Leaves • Can't Smile Without You • Ebony And Ivory • Midnight Cowboy • More • Riders In The Sky • Sentimental Journey • She Touched Me • Stormy Weather • You Don't Bring Me Flowers • and much more.

BROADWAY DELUXE 00309245
126 Smash Broadway songs including: Cabaret • Edelweiss • I Could Have Danced All Night • Memory • Send In The Clowns • Seventy Six Trombones • Sunrise, Sunset • Try To Remember • What Kind Of Fool Am I? • A Wonderful Guy • and many, many more.

CONTEMPORARY HIT DUETS 00359501
14 hit duets from today's biggest pop stars includes Don't Go Breaking My Heart • Endless Love • Ebony And Ivory • Say, Say, Say • You Don't Bring Me Flowers • and more.

CONTEMPORARY LOVE SONGS 00359496
A collection of today's best love songs including Endless Love • September Morn • Feelings • Through The Years • and more.

80's GOLD UPDATE 00359740
Over 70 Hits from the 80's including: All Through The Night • Endless Love • Every Breath You Take • Fortress Around Your Heart • Memory • Miami Vice • One Night In Bangkok • Sentimental Street • What's Love Got To Do With It • Total Eclipse Of The Heart • and more!

FAVORITE HAWAIIAN SONGS 00359852
30 island favorites including Aloha Oe • One Paddle, Two Paddle • Red Sails In The Sunset • Tiny Bubbles • and many more.

GOLDEN ENCYCLOPEDIA OF FOLK MUSIC 00359905
A giant collection of more than 180 classic folk songs including songs of true love, unrequited and false love, spirituals, songs of the west, jolly reunions, international songs and singing the blues.

GRANDMA MOSES SONGBOOK 00359938
A beautiful collection of over 80 traditional and folk songs highlighted by the fascinating paintings of Grandma Moses. Features: America The Beautiful • The Glow Worm • Honeysuckle Rose • I'll Be Home On Christmas Day • Look To The Rainbow • Suddenly There's A Valley • Sunrise, Sunset • Try To Remember • and many, many more!

No. 1 SONGS OF THE 80's 00310666
Arthur's Theme • Everything She Wants • Everytime You Go Away • Careless Whisper • Sailing • What's Love Got To Do With It • The Reflex • Time After Time • and more.

#1 SONGS FROM THE 70's & 80's 00310665
60 of the top songs from the Billboard Hot 100 charts of the 70's and 80's, featuring: Every Breath You Take • How Deep Is Your Love • Joy To The World • Laughter In The Rain • Love Will Keep Us Together • Love's Theme • Maneater • Maniac • Morning Train • Stayin' Alive • and more.

150 OF THE MOST BEAUTIFUL SONGS EVER
Perfect Bound - 00360735   Plastic Comb Bound - 00360734
Bali Ha'i • Bewitched • Could I Have This Dance • I Remember It Well • I'll Be Seeing You • If I Ruled The World • Love Is Blue • Memory • Songbird • When I Need You • and more.

ROCK ON! 00360932
A collection of 50 top rock hits spanning the decades from the 60's to the present. Includes such rock classics as Free Bird • A Whiter Shade Of Pale • Sunshine Of Your Love • Maggie May • and many, many more.

70 CONTEMPORARY HITS 00361056
A super collection of 70 hits featuring: Every Breath You Take • Time After Time • Memory • Wake Me Up Before You Go-Go • Endless Love • Islands In The Stream • Through The Years • Valotte • and many more.

23 AWARD WINNNG POP HITS 00361385
23 of the best including Don't Cry Out Loud • Flashdance. . . What A Feeling • Memory • You Needed Me • and more.

VIDEO ROCK HITS 00361456
A collection of hits by today's biggest video artists — Cindy Lauper, Twisted Sister, Tina Turner, Wham! and others. 21 songs including: Careless Whisper • Hungry Like The Wolf • She Bop • What's Love Got To Do With It • and many more.

YOUNG AT HEART SONGBOOK 00361820
101 light hearted, fun loving favorites: Alley Cat • Bandstand Boogie • Bye Bye Blues • Five Foot Two, Eyes Of Blue • I Could Have Danced All Night • Let Me Entertain You • The Sound Of Music • Tiny Bubbles • True Love • Young At Heart • and more.

ALSO AVAILABLE. . .

HAL LEONARD CHARTBUSTER SERIES
frequently released books of chart songs which include the top recorded hits from Billboard's Top 100 Chart.

PIANO ALPHABETICAL SONGFINDER 72000004
Complete listing of the thousands of songs included in the Easy Piano and Piano/Vocal/Guitar books. Song titles are cross-referenced to the books in which they can be found. Available free of charge from your local music store. Or, write to:
HAL LEONARD PUBLISHING CORP.
P.O. Box 13819, Milwaukee, WI 53213

For more information, contact your local music dealer, or write directly to:

HAL LEONARD PUBLISHING CORPORATION
8112 West Bluemound Rd. P.O. Box 13819 Milwaukee, WI 53213